DISCOURSE

HAND BOOK FOR MASTER AND UNDERGRADUATE STUDENTS.

By

Michael Eury

Table of content:

Printed in the USA.
First Printing, 2023.
Amazon.kdp.online publishing, USA.

PREFACE

Discourse Analysis Today.
Discourse analysis is a field of study that examines language use in its social context. It is concerned with how people use language to create meaning, construct identities, and negotiate power relations. Today, discourse analysis is more important than ever, as our world becomes increasingly complex and interconnected.

This book provides an overview of the main concepts and approaches in discourse analysis, with a focus on contemporary issues and debates. It examines the ways in which discourse shapes and is shaped by social structures and relations, and how it can be used to create and maintain power imbalances.

The book also explores the practical applications of discourse analysis, from political campaigns to media representation to organizational communication. It provides readers with the tools they need to conduct their own discourse analysis, including a step-by-step guide to the research process and examples of different types of data analysis.
Ultimately, this book is a call to action for readers to critically examine the language used in their own lives and the world around them. By understanding the power of discourse, we can become more effective communicators and active participants in shaping our society.

An introduction .
Discourse analysis is a field of study that examines language use in social interactions, focusing on the structures, functions, and meanings of spoken and

written communication. In today's society, discourse analysis has become increasingly important as a tool for understanding the complex ways in which language is used in different contexts, including politics, media, and everyday life.

In this book on discourse analysis today, we will explore various theoretical and methodological approaches to the study of discourse, including conversation analysis, critical discourse analysis, and multimodal discourse analysis. We will also examine the role of discourse in constructing social identities, relationships, and power dynamics, and how it can be used to challenge dominant discourses and promote social change.

Through a range of case studies and examples, this book will demonstrate how discourse analysis can shed light on a variety of issues, from the ways in which media representations shape public opinion, to the impact of language on our perceptions of gender, race, and social class. By the end of the book, readers will have gained a deeper understanding of the complexities of language use in contemporary society, and the potential for discourse analysis to contribute to a more critical and reflective approach to communication.

Discourse Analysis Basics

Discourse analysis definitions and concepts

Discourse analysis is a field of study that focuses on the analysis of language use in social interactions. It seeks to understand how language is used in different contexts, how it shapes and is shaped by social practices and power relations, and how it reflects and reproduces cultural and ideological values. Here are some key definitions and concepts in discourse analysis:

Discourse: Discourse refers to any use of language that occurs in a social context. This includes spoken and written language, as well as other forms of communication such as gestures, facial expressions, and visual media.
Context: The context of discourse refers to the social, cultural, historical, and institutional factors that influence the production and interpretation of language. This includes the physical setting, the participants' identities and roles, the power relations between them, and the larger social and cultural norms and practices.
Power: Power refers to the ability to influence or control others. In discourse analysis, power is seen as inherent in language use, as certain discourses may be used to legitimize or delegitimize certain beliefs, values, and actions.
Ideology: Ideology refers to the system of beliefs, values, and ideas that underlie

social practices and institutions. In discourse analysis, ideology is seen as reflected in language use, as certain discourses may reproduce and reinforce dominant ideological positions.

Discourse community: A discourse community refers to a group of people who share a common set of discursive practices and understandings. Members of a discourse community may use specialized terminology, shared knowledge, and common assumptions to communicate with each other.

Discourse analysis methods: Discourse analysis uses a range of methods to analyze language use, including content analysis, conversation analysis, critical discourse analysis, and multimodal analysis. These methods may involve examining the linguistic features of discourse, analyzing patterns of interaction, and exploring the social and cultural contexts of language use.

Discourse analysis is a broad field with several strands, including the following:
Critical Discourse Analysis (CDA): This approach focuses on the power relations and social structures that are embedded in language use. It aims to uncover the ways in which language is used to maintain or challenge social inequalities. (Fairclough, 1995)

Conversation Analysis (CA): This strand of discourse analysis is concerned with the structure and organization of talk in everyday conversation. It examines how speakers coordinate their turns, repair misunderstandings, and achieve coherence in their interactions. (Sacks, Schegloff, & Jefferson, 1974)
Narrative Analysis: This approach examines the ways in which stories are constructed and told. It looks at the structure of narratives, the characters and events that are included, and the

social and cultural contexts in which they are produced and interpreted. (Labov, 1972)

Discursive Psychology: This strand of discourse analysis focuses on the psychological processes involved in language use. It examines how speakers use language to construct and negotiate their identities, beliefs, and emotions. (Edwards & Potter, 1992)

Multimodal Discourse Analysis (MDA): This approach is concerned with the analysis of different modes of communication, including language, images, and gestures. It examines the ways in which different modes are combined to create meaning in a particular context. (Kress & van Leeuwen, 2001)

Theories of discourse analysis

Discourse analysis is a multidisciplinary field that focuses on the study of language use in social contexts. There are several theories of discourse analysis, each of which emphasizes different aspects of language use and its social functions. Here are a few prominent theories of discourse analysis, along with their respective proponents and some examples of their application:

Critical Discourse Analysis (CDA) - Fairclough (2001) defines CDA as "a type of discourse analytical research that primarily studies the way social power abuse, dominance, and inequality are enacted, reproduced, and resisted by text and talk in the social and political context". CDA aims to uncover hidden power structures and ideologies in discourse by analyzing the ways in which language is used to construct social reality. For example, Van Dijk (1993) analyzed news articles about immigration to show how the media portrays immigrants as a threat to national security, thus reinforcing dominant narratives of exclusion.

Conversation Analysis (CA) - Sacks, Schegloff, and Jefferson (1974) founded CA, which is a theory that studies the organization of talk in everyday social interactions. CA examines how people use language to achieve social actions such as making requests, giving orders, and expressing opinions. For example, Heritage (1984) analyzed doctor-patient interactions to show how doctors use questions to elicit information from patients and how patients use narratives to provide information.

Discursive Psychology (DP) - Potter and Wetherell (1987) founded DP, which is a theory that examines how language is used to construct social reality and identity. DP examines how people use language to construct social categories, such as gender, race, and class, and how these categories are negotiated in social interactions. For example, Billig (1999) analyzed how newspaper articles constructed the category of "Muslim" as a threat to Western civilization.

Speech Act Theory (SAT) - Austin (1962) and Searle (1969) developed SAT, which is a theory that examines how language is used to perform social actions, such as making promises, requests, and apologies. SAT examines how language is used to create social realities and relationships. For example, Brown and Levinson (1987) analyzed the ways in which politeness is used in language to maintain social relationships and avoid conflict.

These are just a few of the many theories of discourse analysis. Each theory offers a unique perspective on language use and its social functions, and all have contributed to our understanding of the role of language in shaping social reality.

Discourse analysis is an interdisciplinary field that examines the ways in which language is used to construct social realities, identities, and relationships. There are several theories of discourse analysis that provide different perspectives on how language works in social interaction. Here are some of the main theories of discourse analysis:

Structuralism: This theory of discourse analysis sees language as a system of signs that are organized according to rules of syntax and grammar. It emphasizes the importance of the relationship between signifiers and signifieds, and how they combine to create meaning.

Post-structuralism: This theory of discourse analysis challenges the idea that language is a stable and fixed system of signs. Instead, it argues that language is constantly changing and that meaning is not fixed but rather depends on the

context in which it is used. It emphasizes the role of power and ideology in shaping discourse.
Critical discourse analysis: This theory of discourse analysis is concerned with how language is used to reproduce and maintain social inequality and power relations. It examines the ways in which discourse reinforces dominant social norms and marginalizes marginalized groups.
Conversation analysis: This theory of discourse analysis focuses on the organization of talk in social interaction. It examines the sequential organization of talk and how participants use language to accomplish specific communicative tasks.
Discursive psychology: This theory of discourse analysis emphasizes the ways in which language is used to construct social identities and relationships. It examines how people use language to

make sense of their experiences and to position themselves and others in social relationships.

Ethnomethodology: This theory of discourse analysis examines the ways in which people make sense of their social world through everyday practices and interactions. It emphasizes the importance of understanding the social context in which language is used and how it is used to construct social realities.
Cooperative Principles:
The Cooperative Principles are a set of principles proposed by philosopher Paul Grice that underlie effective communication in conversation. The four maxims of the Cooperative Principles are:

Maxim of Quantity: The speaker should provide just enough information to

convey their message, without providing too little or too much information.
Example: A customer asks a waiter for the menu. The waiter provides the menu but also adds unnecessary information about the history of the restaurant.

Maxim of Quality: The speaker should only say what they believe to be true and have adequate evidence for, and not say anything that they believe to be false or lacking evidence for.
Example: During a job interview, the candidate is asked about their qualifications and experience. The candidate exaggerates their qualifications and experience to make themselves appear more impressive.

Maxim of Relation: The speaker should stay on topic and make sure their contribution is relevant to the conversation.

Example: During a group discussion about climate change, someone starts talking about their weekend plans, which are unrelated to the topic.
Maxim of Manner: The speaker should be clear, brief, and orderly in their delivery of the message.
Example: During a presentation, the speaker uses technical jargon that the audience doesn't understand, making the presentation unclear and difficult to follow.

Conversational Implicatures:

Conversational implicatures are the meanings conveyed indirectly through speech, based on the context and the speaker's intentions. These meanings are not explicitly stated but can be inferred by the listener. There are two types of conversational implicatures:

conventional implicatures and particularized implicatures.

Conventional Implicatures:

Conventional implicatures are meanings that are conveyed by the use of certain words or phrases in a sentence, regardless of the context. They are not part of the literal meaning of the words, but are implied by the speaker's use of the words.

Example: When someone says "John is a bachelor", the conventional implicature is that John is unmarried.

Particularized Implicatures:

Particularized implicatures are meanings that are conveyed by the context in which a word or phrase is used, as well as the speaker's intention. They are not part of the literal meaning of the words, but are inferred by the listener based on their knowledge of the context and the speaker's intentions.

Example: When someone says "I saw John yesterday", the particularized implicature may be that the speaker and John have a history or relationship that is relevant to the conversation.

Conventional Implicatures:

Conventional implicatures are meanings that are conveyed by the use of certain words or phrases in a sentence, regardless of the context. They are not part of the literal meaning of the words, but are implied by the speaker's use of the words.

Example: When someone says "John is a bachelor", the conventional implicature is that John is unmarried.

Particularized Implicatures:

Particularized implicatures are meanings that are conveyed by the context in which a word or phrase is used, as well as the speaker's intention. They are not part of the literal meaning of the words, but are inferred by the listener based on their

knowledge of the context and the speaker's intentions.
Example: When someone says "I saw John yesterday", the particularized implicature may be that the speaker and John have a history or relationship that is relevant to the conversation.

Speech Acts

A speech act is a type of communicative action that aims to achieve a particular effect on the listener or the reader (Searle, 1969). For example, when a speaker says "I promise to be there at 2 pm," they are performing the speech act of promising. Other types of speech acts include requesting, commanding, apologizing, and congratulating, among others (Austin, 1962).
The effectiveness of a speech act depends not only on the words used but also on the context in which they are uttered

(Bach & Harnish, 1979). For instance, if a police officer says to a driver, "Would you mind stepping out of the car?" the same words spoken in a different context, such as a social gathering, would not be interpreted as a request but as an invitation.

In conclusion, understanding the different types of speech acts and their context-dependent nature can help us communicate more effectively and avoid misunderstandings in our daily interactions (Sperber & Wilson, 1986).
Speech acts refer to the actions performed by a speaker when using language. These actions can be categorized into different types based on their intended function or effect. Here are some examples of different types of speech acts:
Directives: These are speech acts that are used to get someone to do something.

Examples include requests, commands, and suggestions. For example:
Request: "Could you please pass me the salt?"
Command: "Don't touch that!"
Suggestion: "Why don't we take a walk?"
Expressives: These are speech acts that express the speaker's attitudes, feelings, or emotions. Examples include apologies, congratulations, and condolences. For example:
Apology: "I'm sorry I forgot your birthday."
Congratulations: "Congratulations on your graduation!"
Condolences: "I'm sorry for your loss."
Declaratives: These are speech acts that bring about a change in the world, simply by being uttered. Examples include pronouncing someone married or declaring someone guilty. For example:
Marriage pronouncement: "I now pronounce you husband and wife."

Guilty verdict: "The jury finds the defendant guilty."
Commissives: These are speech acts that commit the speaker to some future course of action. Examples include promises, threats, and offers. For example:
Promise: "I promise I will be there on time."
Threat: "If you don't stop talking, I'm going to leave."
Offer: "Would you like me to help you with that?"
Assertives: These are speech acts that express a belief or judgment. Examples include assertions, denials, and explanations. For example:
Assertion: "The earth revolves around the sun."
Denial: "I didn't take your book."
Explanation: "I was late because there was an accident on the highway."

Speech acts are an important aspect of communication and understanding their different types can help us better understand the intentions behind the words we use and hear.

Politeness and Face Threats

politeness principles and face threatening acts

Politeness principles and face-threatening principles are two related concepts in the field of communication and language.

Politeness principles refer to the social norms and conventions that govern how people interact with each other in order to maintain positive relationships and avoid conflict. The most common politeness principles are:

Tact: avoiding saying things that might be harmful or offensive

Generosity: making others feel valued and respected

Approbation: giving praise and positive feedback
Modesty: downplaying one's own achievements and abilities
Agreement: finding common ground and avoiding disagreement
On the other hand, face-threatening principles refer to situations in which communication can cause damage to someone's face or self-image. This can happen when a message threatens someone's sense of social identity, such as their reputation, self-esteem, or social status. Some common face-threatening principles include:
Criticism: pointing out flaws or mistakes in someone's behavior or performance
Face-threatening acts: actions that challenge someone's autonomy or social position, such as giving orders, making demands, or asking intrusive questions

Threats: communicating a negative consequence if someone does not comply with a request or demand.

In conclusion, while politeness principles aim to promote positive communication and social harmony, face-threatening principles recognize that communication can sometimes be confrontational and that people have a need to protect their face or self-image in these situations. Effective communication requires balancing these two sets of principles to achieve both positive outcomes and avoid unnecessary conflict.

Face threatening acts

Face-threatening acts are actions or messages that challenge someone's social identity, self-image, or autonomy. They can cause damage to someone's face or reputation and lead to negative emotions, such as anger, embarrassment, or shame.

Examples of face-threatening acts include:

Giving orders or commands: When someone is told what to do without being given a choice, it can be seen as a threat to their autonomy and social status.

Criticizing or blaming: When someone is criticized or blamed for something, it can be perceived as a challenge to their competence, character, or integrity.

Disagreeing or contradicting: When someone's ideas or opinions are challenged or contradicted, it can be perceived as a threat to their beliefs or values.

Correcting or instructing: When someone is corrected or instructed on how to do something, it can be perceived as a threat to their knowledge or expertise.

Asking personal or intrusive questions: When someone is asked personal or intrusive questions, it can be perceived as a threat to their privacy or boundaries.

Effective communication requires a balance between politeness principles and face-threatening acts. To minimize face-threatening acts, it's important to use language that is respectful, considerate, and sensitive to the other person's feelings and needs.

Presuppositions in communication

Presupposition is a linguistic concept that refers to an assumption that is made by a speaker or writer about what the listener or reader already knows or believes. In other words, a presupposition is something that is taken for granted or assumed to be true without being explicitly stated.

For example, if someone says, "John stopped smoking," the presupposition is that John was smoking in the past. Similarly, if someone says, "I regret eating that pizza," the presupposition is

that the speaker ate pizza at some point in the past.
Presuppositions can be important in communication because they can affect how a message is received and understood by the listener or reader. They can also be used strategically in certain types of communication, such as persuasion or negotiation, to influence the other party's beliefs or assumptions.
Examples of presuppositions:

"Are you still driving that old car?" - The presupposition is that the listener has an old car.
"Did you enjoy the concert?" - The presupposition is that the listener went to a concert.
"I need to buy more dog food." - The presupposition is that the speaker has a dog.

"Have you stopped cheating on your exams?" - The presupposition is that the listener has been cheating on exams.
"She was disappointed when she found out the party was canceled." - The presupposition is that there was a party scheduled that was later canceled.
"I'm sorry, we're out of that item." - The presupposition is that the listener was trying to buy a specific item.
"I'm not going to argue with you." - The presupposition is that the speaker and listener were having an argument.

Mutual Contextual Beliefs (MCBs)

Mutual contextual beliefs refer to the shared beliefs or assumptions that two or more individuals hold about their social or physical environment. These beliefs are based on their shared experiences and interactions, and are often implicit or taken for granted.

For example, if two individuals have lived in the same neighborhood for a long time, they may share certain beliefs about the safety or quality of life in that neighborhood, based on their shared experiences living there. Or, if two individuals work in the same industry, they may share certain assumptions about how that industry operates, based on their shared experiences working in it. Mutual contextual beliefs are important because they help individuals understand and navigate their social and physical environments. By sharing these beliefs, individuals can establish a common understanding of their surroundings, which can facilitate communication, collaboration, and decision-making.

Here are some examples of mutual contextual beliefs:

Neighborhood safety: Two neighbors who have both lived in the same area for many years may share a mutual contextual belief that their neighborhood is safe because they have not experienced any major crimes or incidents.

Company culture: Two employees who have worked in the same company for a long time may share a mutual contextual belief about the company culture, such as the importance of teamwork or the value placed on work-life balance.

Social norms: Two individuals who grew up in the same cultural or social environment may share a mutual contextual belief about social norms, such as the appropriate way to greet someone or the importance of family values.

Political ideology: Two individuals who belong to the same political party or movement may share a mutual contextual belief about the role of government or the importance of certain policies.

Academic disciplines: Two scholars who work in the same academic discipline may share a mutual contextual belief about the methods and standards of research and scholarship within their field.

Mutual Contextual Beliefs (MCBs)

Mutual Contextual Beliefs (MCBs) refer to shared assumptions or beliefs between individuals about the context or situation in which they are communicating. MCBs can facilitate communication by allowing individuals to make assumptions about what the other person knows or believes, and by providing a shared framework for understanding the conversation. Here are some examples of research studies that have explored MCBs:

In a study by Clark and Marshall (1981), participants were shown a picture of a scene and asked to describe it. The researchers found that participants who had previously discussed the scene with another person were more likely to use MCBs in their descriptions, such as assuming that the other person knew the location of objects in the scene.

In a study by Brennan and Clark (1996), participants were given a set of objects and asked to arrange them in a particular way. The researchers found that participants who were paired with someone they knew well were more likely to use MCBs, such as assuming that the other person knew how to arrange the objects without being explicitly told.

In a study by Brown and Levinson (1987), participants were asked to rate the politeness of different utterances. The researchers found that the perceived politeness of an utterance was influenced by MCBs, such as assuming that the speaker and listener shared the same social norms.

Overall, these studies suggest that MCBs play an important role in communication and can facilitate mutual understanding between individuals.

Inference and Reasoning.

Inference refers to the process of drawing conclusions or making predictions based on evidence, observations, or prior knowledge. Inference involves using reasoning and critical thinking skills to make logical deductions and come to a conclusion.

In various contexts, inference can mean different things. For example, in statistics, inference refers to the process of using data to make conclusions or predictions about a population. In natural language processing, inference refers to the ability of a machine learning model to make predictions based on input data.

In everyday life, inference can be seen in situations where we make educated guesses or assumptions based on what we observe. For instance, we might infer that someone is tired because they are yawning, or we might infer that a storm is coming because the sky is darkening.

Overall, inference is an essential cognitive process that allows us to make sense of the world around us and make decisions based on the available information.

Here are some examples of inference:

Sherlock Holmes is a master of inference. He is able to make deductions and predictions based on seemingly minor details. For example, he might infer that a person is left-handed based on the way they hold their pen, or that a person has traveled recently based on the wear patterns on their shoes.

You see a person running down the street, looking over their shoulder. Based on this observation, you might infer that they are being chased or that they are late for an appointment.

You notice that the ground is wet and there are puddles everywhere. Based on this observation, you might infer that it has been raining recently.

You hear a loud noise coming from your neighbor's apartment. Based on this observation, you might infer that they are moving furniture or that they are having a party.

You are taking a multiple-choice test and notice that all the answers are in the same letter sequence. Based on this observation, you might infer that the test is a pattern-based one.

These examples illustrate how we use inference to draw conclusions or make predictions based on observations, evidence, or prior knowledge.

Text Discourse Features

Text discourse features refer to the linguistic elements present in a text that help to organize and structure the information presented. According to Halliday and Hasan (1976), there are several types of discourse features, including:

Cohesion: This refers to the grammatical and lexical devices used to link the various parts of a text. Examples include reference (e.g. pronouns), substitution (e.g. "it" instead of repeating a noun), ellipsis (e.g. leaving out words that are implied), and conjunction (e.g. "and", "but").

Coherence: This refers to the overall sense of unity and logic that a text conveys. It is achieved through the use of cohesive devices as well as through the organization of information into clear and meaningful patterns.

Genre: This refers to the type of text being produced and the conventions associated with that type. Different genres have different expectations in terms of organization, style, and content.
Intertextuality: This refers to the ways in which a text refers to or is influenced by other texts, either explicitly or implicitly. This can include allusions, quotations, or simply the use of familiar language or ideas.Halliday and Hasan,(1976).
Overall, these discourse features play a crucial role in shaping the way we understand and interpret texts. By using them effectively, writers can create texts that are clear, coherent, and engaging for readers.
Discourse features refer to the ways in which language is used in communication to convey meaning beyond the literal level. These features include things like tone, intonation, register, and rhetorical devices. Here are

some examples of discourse features in text:

Tone: the writer's attitude towards the subject matter, conveyed through word choice and phrasing. For example, in a persuasive essay, the writer might use a tone that is confident and assertive to persuade the reader to agree with their argument.

Intonation: the rise and fall of the writer's voice in speech, which can convey emphasis, emotion, or sarcasm. In written text, intonation can be conveyed through punctuation, such as exclamation marks or question marks.

Register: the level of formality or informality in the language used. For example, a legal document would use a formal register, while a text message between friends might use a more informal register.

Rhetorical devices: techniques used to make language more effective and persuasive, such as repetition, metaphor, or rhetorical questions. For example, a politician might use a rhetorical question to engage the audience and make them think about a particular issue.

Cohesion: the ways in which ideas are connected and linked together in a text, through the use of conjunctions, pronouns, and other linking words. For example, a news article might use a pronoun like "it" to refer back to a previous sentence or idea.

Genre conventions: the expectations and conventions of different types of texts, such as a news article, a novel, or a poem. For example, a poem might use meter and rhyme to create a particular effect or mood.

Here are some examples of discourse features in text:

Tone:

a) Confident and assertive tone in a persuasive essay: "It is clear that the evidence supports our argument. Therefore, it is essential that we take action now."
b) Sarcastic tone in a humorous article: "Oh, great. Another meeting. Just what I wanted to do with my afternoon."
Intonation:
a) Use of an exclamation mark to convey excitement: "I can't wait to see you!"
b) Use of a question mark to convey confusion: "Why did you do that?"
Register:
a) Formal register in a legal document: "Pursuant to section 2.1 of the agreement, the party of the first part shall have the right to terminate this agreement at any time."
b) Informal register in a text message: "Hey, what's up? Wanna grab some pizza later?"
Rhetorical devices:

a) Use of repetition for emphasis: "We will not rest until we have achieved our goal. We will not give up. We will not be defeated."
b) Use of a rhetorical question to engage the audience: "Can we really afford to ignore the plight of the homeless in our city?"
Cohesion:
a) Use of a pronoun to refer back to a previous sentence: "The experiment was successful. It confirmed our hypothesis and showed that it was feasible."
b) Use of a conjunction to link ideas together: "She studied hard for the exam, but she still didn't do very well."
Genre conventions:
a) Use of meter and rhyme in a poem: "I wandered lonely as a cloud / That floats on high o'er vales and hills."
b) Use of descriptive language in a novel: "The sky was a deep shade of blue, and

the sun was just starting to set behind the mountains."

Critical Discourse Analysis (CDA)

Critical Discourse Analysis (CDA) is a theoretical framework that examines the relationship between language, power, and ideology (Fairclough, 1995). It is an interdisciplinary approach that draws on linguistics, sociology, anthropology, and other fields to analyze how language is used to reproduce and maintain power relations in society.

CDA focuses on the ways in which language is used to construct and maintain dominant social ideologies and power structures (Van Dijk, 1993). This includes analyzing the ways in which language is used to marginalize or exclude certain groups, to reinforce stereotypes, and to perpetuate inequality. CDA also looks at how language is used to create and maintain discourses that support particular political, economic, and social interests.

One of the key concepts in CDA is intertextuality, which refers to the ways in which texts are connected to other texts and to the broader social and historical context in which they are produced (Fairclough, 2001). CDA analysts examine how texts are influenced by and contribute to the larger discourses that circulate in society.

Another important concept in CDA is hegemony, which refers to the process by which dominant groups establish and maintain their power over subordinate groups through ideological means (Gramsci, 1971). CDA examines how language is used to reinforce and reproduce hegemonic power relations, and how alternative discourses can challenge and potentially transform these power relations.

Overall, CDA offers a critical perspective on the role of language in shaping social reality, and it provides a framework for analyzing how language is used to maintain or challenge power relations in society.

Critical Discourse Analysis (CDA) is an interdisciplinary approach to the study of language, discourse, and power that aims to analyze how language is used to construct and reproduce social inequalities, ideologies, and power relations. Here are some examples of CDA:

Media discourse: CDA can be used to analyze media discourse and how it constructs and reinforces dominant ideologies and power relations. For example, a CDA study of news coverage of immigration might analyze how language is used to construct immigrants as criminals or threats to national security, reinforcing dominant narratives of nationalism and xenophobia.

Political discourse: CDA can also be used to analyze political discourse and how language is used to construct political identities and power relations. For example, a CDA study of political speeches might analyze how language is used to construct a particular political party or leader as legitimate and authoritative, while others are constructed as illegitimate or inferior.

Education discourse: CDA can also be used to analyze education discourse and how language is used to construct and reinforce social hierarchies and power relations in education. For example, a CDA study of textbooks might analyze how language is used to construct certain groups as superior or inferior, or how language is used to reinforce gender stereotypes in education.

Advertising discourse: CDA can also be used to analyze advertising discourse and how language is used to construct and reinforce gender, racial, and other social stereotypes. For example, a CDA study of advertising might analyze how language is used to construct women as objects of desire or men as dominant and powerful, reinforcing gender stereotypes and power relations in society.

Overall, CDA is a powerful tool for analyzing how language is used to construct and reinforce social inequalities, ideologies, and power relations in various contexts.

Here are some more specific examples of CDA:

A CDA analysis of a political campaign speech might examine how the candidate uses language to construct their political identity and to create a sense of belonging and trust with their audience. This might involve analyzing the use of metaphors, rhetorical devices, and linguistic patterns to create a particular tone or style of communication.

A CDA analysis of a news article might examine how the language used to report on an event reinforces or challenges existing power structures and ideologies. For example, a CDA analysis of news coverage of protests might examine how language is used to construct protestors as either legitimate or illegitimate, or how language is used to create a sense of moral panic or urgency around the issue at hand.

A CDA analysis of a social media platform might examine how language and design features are used to construct and reinforce particular norms and values within the community. This might involve analyzing the use of emojis, hashtags, and other linguistic or visual cues to create a sense of belonging or to signal membership in a particular group.

A CDA analysis of a workplace policy document might examine how language is used to construct and reinforce hierarchies and power relations within the organization. This might involve analyzing the use of passive voice, technical jargon, and other linguistic strategies to create a sense of distance or authority between different levels of the organizational hierarchy.

Overall, CDA can be applied to a wide range of language use contexts to uncover the ways in which language is used to create and reinforce power relations and social inequalities.Critical discourse of a picture displaying politicians on both side and insecurity in the middle

The picture you described, depicting politicians on both sides and insecurity in the middle, can be interpreted in a number of ways. Here is one possible critical discourse:

At first glance, the image seems to suggest a political divide, with two opposing factions facing off against each other. However, the real focus of the picture is the insecurity in the middle, which is represented by a range of different symbols.

This insecurity could represent a number of different issues that are facing society today. For example, it might symbolize the growing divide between the rich and poor, the rising threat of climate change, or the increasing levels of political polarization.

One possible interpretation of the image is that it is a commentary on the failure of politicians to address these pressing issues. Instead of coming together to find solutions, they are depicted as being locked in a perpetual struggle for power and control. In doing so, they are neglecting the needs of the people who they are supposed to serve, and exacerbating the insecurity that is plaguing society.

Another possible interpretation of the image is that it represents the need for a new kind of politics, one that is focused on bridging the divide between different groups and addressing the underlying causes of insecurity. This might involve building coalitions between different interest groups, promoting dialogue and understanding, and seeking out innovative solutions to the challenges that we face.

Ultimately, the picture can be seen as a call to action, urging us to recognize the deep-seated insecurities that are affecting our world today and to work towards a more inclusive, compassionate, and sustainable future.

Discourse stylistics

Discourse stylistics is the study of how language is used in texts to convey meaning and achieve particular effects. It looks at the ways in which writers use different linguistic features such as grammar, vocabulary, tone, and rhetorical devices to create their intended effect on the reader.

Stylistics of Discourse.

Discourse stylistics refers to the study of the ways in which language is used in different contexts and situations to convey meaning and create particular effects. It encompasses various aspects of language use such as grammar, vocabulary, syntax, and rhetorical devices..

One important aspect of discourse stylistics is the use of rhetorical devices, which are linguistic tools that help speakers or writers achieve particular communicative goals. These devices include figures of speech such as metaphor, simile, personification, hyperbole, and irony. For example, in his famous "I Have a Dream" speech, Martin Luther King Jr. used a range of rhetorical devices to convey his message of racial equality and justice. One example is the use of metaphors, such as "the sweltering heat of injustice" and "the oasis of freedom and justice." These metaphors create vivid images in the listener's mind and help to reinforce the message of the speech (King, 1963).

Another important element of discourse stylistics is the use of cohesive devices, which are linguistic features that help to link different parts of a text together and create coherence. Cohesive devices include pronouns, conjunctions, lexical repetition, and reference markers. For example, in a news article reporting on a political event, the use of pronouns such as "he" and "she" can help to clarify who is being referred to and maintain coherence throughout the article. Similarly, the use of reference markers such as "the former president" and "the current administration" can help to establish continuity and coherence in a text.

Finally, discourse stylistics also encompasses the use of register, which refers to the level of formality and the social context in which language is used. Different registers are appropriate for different situations and contexts, and speakers and writers need to be able to adjust their language use accordingly. For example, the language used in a formal academic article will be quite different from the language used in an informal chat with friends. Register can also be influenced by factors such as audience, purpose, and genre.

In conclusion, discourse stylistics is a complex and multifaceted area of study that encompasses a range of linguistic features and communicative goals. By understanding the different elements of discourse stylistics and how they are used in different contexts, we can gain a deeper appreciation for the richness and complexity of language use.

Here are some examples of discourse stylistics:

Metaphor: "She was a shining star in his dark world."

Metaphor is a figure of speech in which a word or phrase is applied to an object or action to which it is not literally applicable. In the example above, the metaphorical use of the phrase "shining star" creates an image of brightness and hope in contrast to the darkness of the world.

Irony: "Thanks for the ticket officer, you just made my day."
Irony is the use of language to convey a meaning that is the opposite of its literal meaning. In this example, the speaker is being sarcastic by thanking the officer for giving them a ticket, which is usually considered a negative thing.
Repetition: "I have a dream that one day this nation will rise up and live out the true meaning of its creed: 'We hold these truths to be self-evident, that all men are created equal.'"
Repetition is the repeated use of a word or phrase for emphasis. In this example, Martin Luther King Jr. repeats the phrase "I have a dream" and the phrase "all men are created equal" to emphasize his vision of racial equality.
Personification: "The wind whispered through the trees."
Personification is a figure of speech in which a non-human object is given

human-like qualities. In this example, the wind is personified as if it has the ability to whisper, which creates an image of a gentle breeze blowing through the trees.

Alliteration: "Peter Piper picked a peck of pickled peppers."

Alliteration is the repetition of consonant sounds at the beginning of words. In this example, the repeated "p" sound creates a rhythmic pattern and draws attention to the tongue-twister nature of the sentence.

Hyperbole: "I've told you a million times to clean your room!"

Hyperbole is the use of exaggeration for emphasis or effect. In this example, the speaker uses hyperbole to emphasize the number of times they have asked the person to clean their room, even though they haven't actually asked that many times.

Onomatopoeia: "The bees buzzed around the flowers."
Onomatopoeia is the use of words that imitate the sound of the thing they describe. In this example, the word "buzzed" imitates the sound of the bees flying around the flowers.Here are some additional examples of discourse stylistics:

Assonance: "Hear the mellow wedding bells."
Assonance is the repetition of vowel sounds within words. In this example, the repeated "e" sound in "mellow" and "wedding" creates a musical effect.
Juxtaposition: "It was the best of times, it was the worst of times."
Juxtaposition is the placement of two contrasting ideas or images side by side. In this example, Charles Dickens uses juxtaposition to contrast the best and

worst of times, highlighting the extremes of the time period he is describing.
Rhetorical question: "What's in a name? That which we call a rose by any other name would smell as sweet."
A rhetorical question is a question asked for effect, rather than to elicit an answer. In this example, Shakespeare uses a rhetorical question to explore the idea that a name doesn't affect the inherent qualities of an object, in this case a rose.
Imagery: "The sun was setting, casting a golden glow over the ocean."
Imagery is the use of language to create a sensory experience for the reader. In this example, the image of the sun setting and casting a golden glow over the ocean creates a vivid visual picture in the reader's mind.

Parallelism: "Ask not what your country can do for you, ask what you can do for your country."

Parallelism is the use of grammatically similar phrases or clauses for emphasis. In this example, John F. Kennedy uses parallelism to emphasize the idea of civic responsibility and encourage individuals to contribute to their country.

Anaphora: "I have a dream that one day...I have a dream that one day...I have a dream that one day..."
Anaphora is the repetition of a word or phrase at the beginning of successive clauses or sentences. In this example, Martin Luther King Jr. uses anaphora to emphasize his dream of racial equality and create a rhythmic effect in his speech.
Allusion: "He was a real Romeo with the ladies."
Allusion is a reference to a well-known person, place, event, or literary work. In this example, the speaker uses the allusion to Romeo, the romantic hero of

Shakespeare's play, to convey that the man in question is charming and a ladies' man.Here are some more examples of discourse stylistics:
Euphemism: "He passed away peacefully in his sleep."
Euphemism is the use of a milder, indirect, or vague term to refer to something that may be considered unpleasant, offensive, or taboo. In this example, the euphemism "passed away" is used instead of "died" to soften the impact of the news.
Antithesis: "It was the best of times, it was the worst of times."
Antithesis is the use of contrasting ideas, words, or phrases within a parallel grammatical structure. In this example, the phrase "best of times" is contrasted with "worst of times," creating a sense of tension and highlighting the extremes of the time period being described.
Litotes: "She's not unkind."

Litotes is a figure of speech in which an idea is expressed by negating its opposite. In this example, the phrase "not unkind" is used to convey that the person is actually kind, without using a direct statement.

Chiasmus: "Ask not what your country can do for you, ask what you can do for your country."

Chiasmus is a figure of speech in which the order of words or phrases in the first clause is reversed in the second clause. In this example, the order of "your country" and "you" is reversed in the second clause, creating a balanced and memorable sentence.

Synecdoche: "All hands on deck."

Synecdoche is a figure of speech in which a part of something is used to represent the whole, or vice versa. In this example, "hands" is used to represent the entire crew of a ship.

Zeugma: "He lost his keys and his temper."
Zeugma is a figure of speech in which a verb is used to apply to two different objects in different ways. In this example, the verb "lost" is used to describe both the physical loss of keys and the emotional loss of temper.
Hyperbole: "I've told you a million times!"
Hyperbole is the use of exaggeration for emphasis or effect. In this example, the speaker uses hyperbole to emphasize that they have told the listener something many times, even though it is unlikely that they have literally told them a million times.
Irony: "Water, water everywhere, but not a drop to drink."
Irony is the use of words that convey a meaning opposite to their literal or expected meaning. In this example, the phrase "water, water everywhere"

suggests an abundance of water, but the phrase "not a drop to drink" reveals the ironic truth that the water is actually undrinkable.

Metaphor: "Life is a journey."

Metaphor is a figure of speech that uses one thing to represent another thing in order to create an image or comparison. In this example, the metaphor compares life to a journey, highlighting the idea that life involves a series of experiences and changes over time.

Oxymoron: "Jumbo shrimp"

An oxymoron is a figure of speech that combines two contradictory terms to create a new meaning. In this example, the term "jumbo shrimp" combines the idea of something large and something small, creating a playful and paradoxical effect.

Personification: "The wind whispered in my ear."

Personification is the attribution of human characteristics to nonhuman things or abstract concepts. In this example, the wind is personified as whispering, creating a sensory image and enhancing the emotional impact of the sentence.
Simile: "Her eyes shone like diamonds."
Simile is a figure of speech that uses "like" or "as" to compare two things. In this example, the simile compares the brightness and clarity of the woman's eyes to diamonds, creating a vivid image for the reader.
Understatement: "I'm just a little bit tired."
Understatement is the use of language that minimizes the impact of a situation or event. In this example, the speaker uses understatement to downplay their fatigue, making the situation seem less serious than it actually is.

Conclusion. In conclusion, discourse analysis is a vital tool in understanding and analyzing the ways in which language is used to construct meaning, shape social realities, and produce power relations in contemporary society. This book has provided an in-depth exploration of the key concepts and methodologies of discourse analysis, as well as the various theoretical frameworks that underpin this approach. Through the use of practical examples and case studies, this book has demonstrated how discourse analysis can be applied in a range of contexts, from political speeches and media representations to everyday interactions and social media discourses. It has also highlighted the importance of considering the socio-political context in which language is produced and consumed, and the role that discourse plays in reinforcing or challenging dominant power relations.

Overall, this book has shown that discourse analysis is a dynamic and constantly evolving field, which offers a powerful lens through which to examine the complex ways in which language shapes our understanding of the world around us. By encouraging critical reflection on the language we use and the discourses we encounter, discourse analysis has the potential to promote more nuanced and inclusive forms of communication and social interaction.

References:

Fairclough, N. (1995). Critical discourse analysis: The critical study of language. Longman.

Fairclough, N. (2001). Language and power. Pearson Education.

Gramsci, A. (1971). Selections from the Prison Notebooks. Lawrence and Wishart.
Van Dijk, T. A. (1993). Principles of critical discourse analysis. Discourse and society, 4(2), 249-283.
Fairclough, N. (1995). Critical discourse analysis: The critical study of language. Routledge.
Sacks, H., Schegloff, E. A., & Jefferson, G. (1974). A simplest systematics for the organization of turn-taking for conversation. Language, 50(4), 696-735.
Labov, W. (1972). Language in the inner city: Studies in the Black English Vernacular. University of Pennsylvania Press.
Edwards, D., & Potter, J. (1992). Discursive psychology. Sage Publications.
Kress, G., & van Leeuwen, T. (2001). Multimodal discourse: The modes and media of contemporary communication. Arnold.

King, M. L. (1963). I Have a Dream. Speech delivered at the Lincoln Memorial, Washington D.C. August 28, 1963.
Gee, J. P. (2014). An introduction to discourse analysis: Theory and method (4th ed.). Routledge.
Fairclough, N. (2015). Language and power (3rd ed.). Routledge.
Wodak, R., & Meyer, M. (Eds.). (2015). Methods of critical discourse studies (3rd ed.). Sage.
van Dijk, T. A. (2017). Discourse and context: A sociocognitive approach. Cambridge University Press.
Schiffrin, D., Tannen, D., & Hamilton, H. E. (Eds.). (2001). The handbook of discourse analysis. Blackwell Publishers.
Stubbs, M. (2017). Discourse analysis: An introduction (2nd ed.). Routledge.
Jørgensen, M., & Phillips, L. J. (Eds.). (2002). Discourse analysis as theory and method. Sage.

Coulthard, M. (2004). Advances in spoken discourse analysis. Routledge.
Potter, J., & Wetherell, M. (2013). Discourse and social psychology: Beyond attitudes and behavior (2nd ed.). Sage.
Edwards, D., & Potter, J. (1992). Discursive psychology. Sage.

•

Printed in Great Britain
by Amazon

26080184R00046